Original title:
Songbirds of the Cedars

Copyright © 2025 Creative Arts Management OÜ
All rights reserved.

Author: Christian Leclair
ISBN HARDBACK: 978-1-80567-297-5
ISBN PAPERBACK: 978-1-80567-596-9

Ethereal Echoes of The Wanderers

In the trees they flap and chatter,
With a style that always matters,
Feathers bright, they prance, jovial,
Creating sounds almost royal.

Their notes jump like a bouncy ball,
Echoing across the forest hall,
Wings like feathers, in a race,
Chasing laughter, a merry chase.

Hopping, flapping, what a sight!
Dancing 'neath the morning light,
Beaks all bobbing with great flair,
Do they even have a care?

In the pines they play their tunes,
Causing giggles from the moons,
Life a party, skies all clear,
With these jesters, who will steer?

Songs Carried by the Breeze

In the trees, a chirp on high,
A wee bird hops, oh my, oh my!
With wings like socks, it flits around,
Spreading giggles, silly sound.

It steals a snack, a berry sweet,
Chasing ants on little feet.
Dancing leaves join in the fun,
As sunlight bathes everyone!

Symphonic Elegance amid the Pines

A feathered friend with fancy flair,
Wobbles on the branch with care.
It sings a tune, or does a jig,
A sight to see, a lively gig!

With every note, the trees do sway,
As critters stop to watch the play.
A concert grand beneath the sky,
Where every giggle makes us sigh.

The Melodic Greenthroat

In plaid and polka dots so bright,
A greenthroat croons with all its might.
It tells just jokes, no songs of woe,
While squirrels chuckle, laughing so!

On branches high, it reigns supreme,
With humor mixed in every dream.
A tuning fork on nature's stage,
Whimsical fun, all the rage!

Whispers in the Woodland Wind

In rustling leaves, the gossip flows,
Of feathered friends and silly woes.
An owl misheard a joke last night,
Now every creature takes delight.

The wild breeze carries laughter near,
As frolicsome tales we hold dear.
A chorus born from frolic sore,
In woods alive with laughter's roar!

Poetry on the Wind's Breath

Fluttering flaps in the bright blue sky,
Chasing each other with a cheeky fly.
A worm does the tango, so easy to spy,
But it's all just a prank—a worm with a tie!

They chirp little jokes, with a wink and a grin,
Hiding their giggles, it's such a wild spin.
Perched on a branch, they let the fun begin,
A feathery party, no one's wearing skin!

Harmonies of the Wandering Winds

A gust sweeps in, ruffling their feathers,
They sing of the weather—oh, how it fetters!
Bouncing on breezes like they're on tethers,
Whipping up laughter, and gales that are betters!

One blurted a tune that made the others squawk,
A dance off begins, with a raucous talk.
They shimmy and shake, and then they just rock,
Even the squirrels stop to gawk at the flock!

Chiming in the Cedar's Embrace

In the arms of the tree, they flit and they sway,
A raucous assembly, in a feathery way.
Each note is a chuckle, with the sun's bright ray,
They tickle the branches, turning work into play!

A cheeky young finch tried to steal the show,
By throwing a twig like a fast-moving bow.
But it landed a flump, not quite with the flow,
And the chorus erupted in giggles aglow!

Trills Above the Trampled Trail

Up where the timid hikers step with care,
A ruckus erupts from the bramble and air.
With trills and with quips, they dance everywhere,
Making the trodden path feel like a fair!

One bold little bird took a dive and a twirl,
Pretending to slip, giving all a strong whirl.
But his buddies just laughed, what an avian pearl,
As they pranced in the breeze, every feather a swirl!

Whispers Among the Evergreens

In the trees, a parrot squeaks,
A squirrel nods, the woodpecker peeks.
They gossip 'bout the acorns' fate,
While a raccoon arrives too late.

A chipmunk sings a silly tune,
With a rabbit dancing under the moon.
The owls roll their eyes, say 'Oh dear!',
As the deer join in, drinking their beer.

Melodies in the Mist

A crow misreads the morning call,
Ends up singing at the wrong mall.
The fog giggles as it hides the sun,
While frogs argue who's the best one.

Down by the brook, a finch tumbles,
Tripping over roots, it stumbles.
The twilight chorus starts its blend,
As the raccoons dance, they just pretend.

Echoes Beneath the Branches

In the shade, a lizard plays the flute,
While chipmunks wear tiny boots.
Rabbits hop on their hind legs too,
Wondering why the sky's so blue.

A nightingale's missed its chance,
Singing solo at a squirrel's dance.
A beehive swings to the funky beat,
And ants try to join, but can't find their feet.

Harmonies of the Woodland

The wind carries a hiccuped song,
A frog croaks out, 'Can't be wrong!'
The trees sway, laughing in delight,
While a hedgehog rolls into the night.

Chirps and tweets, a bat throws shade,
As the fireflies join the parade.
Through branches thick, the echoes play,
Nature's choir in a goofy display.

Crescendos in the Conifer

In the branches, voices sing,
Chirps and caws, a merry fling.
Twigs dance wildly to the sound,
Nature's disco all around.

Feathers flop in silly flight,
Squawking jokes from dawn till night.
A raucous band, they take the stage,
With banter that will never age.

Nature's Call and Response

One chirps out a funny tune,
Another joins, a silly swoon.
They tease each other, plucky birds,
With puns and quips, despite their words.

The trees go laughing, roots in glee,
As feathered jesters shout with glee.
Echoes bounce from trunk to bough,
Nature's chatter—oh, what a show!

Canorous Echoes through the Foliage

Up above, a chorus bursts,
A cacophony of quirky thirsts.
Little birds with big old dreams,
Hatching plans as bright as beams.

They chirp of worms and silly games,
Of flying high and dodging flames.
Their laughter rustles leaves anew,
With every note, a chuckle grew.

Melodic Whispers from Above

A light breeze carries laughter near,
As tiny birds sing loud and clear.
With twirls and dips, they take a bow,
Their wit more sharp than any plow.

What tales they weave in vibrant air,
Of wormy feasts and feathered flair.
In every note, a jest is spun,
In this woodland, life's just fun!

Fluttering Voices at Dusk

Tiny wings in leafy nests,
Chirping loud like little pests.
Fluffy feathers, round and bright,
Tweeting tales that end in flight.

With a hop, they steal the show,
Singing off-key, putting on a glow.
Dancing on branches, oh what a sight,
Making the dusk a giggling delight.

Choral Reflections in the Glade

In the glade, they hold a feast,
Merry notes from west to east.
One sings high, the other low,
A funny duet, as it turns out so!

With a wink and a tail flip,
They line up for a harmony trip.
Bouncing notes on springs of glee,
Laughing skills of pure parody.

Dawn Chorus of the Hidden Glen

At dawn, they wake with a start,
Warbling tunes that sound like art.
Chirps and cheeps shoot through the air,
Funny faces showing their flair.

A ruffled crew with silly beaks,
Tickling brambles, sharing sneaks.
Each note a wink, each call a laugh,
Nature's jesters in their own staff.

Rhythms of the Rustic Grove

Rustic dorms in trees so tall,
Echoing giggles as they squall.
Every branch becomes a stage,
As they perform in a rustic rage.

Tapping feet on twigs with glee,
Their antics spark joy for all to see.
Chirping rounds, all offbeat,
An orchestra where laughs compete.

The Airborne Ballad

Up in the trees, a ruckus reigns,
Feathers and flutters, it never wanes.
The chirps are like jokes, a natural quirk,
While squirrels roll their eyes, 'Oh, that's just their perk.'

Each twist of a wing sends a giggle around,
The prancing of branches, a dance unbound.
With beaks full of berries, they plot and conspire,
A comedy show, that never grows tired.

Chants from the Canopy

In the leafy dome, a chorus unfolds,
With silly remarks that the crow often scolds.
The finch with a grin, does a flip and a flop,
While the owl simply yawns, 'Why can't they just stop?'

A warbler croons tunes about worms in the dirt,
With a twist and a twirl, he's a clumsy expert.
Laughter rustles softly through branches so wide,
As the chattering crew takes their whimsy in stride.

The Rustling Rhymes

In a tangle of leaves, the songs intertwine,
With laughs echoing, it's a silly design.
The thrush sings a ballad of berries so bright,
While the jay cackles loud, 'I could snack here all night!'

With each little hop, they spread joy and cheer,
Squeaking out jokes that no one seems to hear.
A procession of flutters, their antics a sight,
Creating a ruckus from morning till night.

Hymns of the Meadow's Breath

In the meadow, they gather, a mischievous squad,
With nonsense they bicker, and chirp for a nod.
The lark takes the lead in a wild parody,
While the woodpecker knocks in absurdity.

Amidst wildflowers, they share tales so bright,
Of mishaps and blunders that tickle with light.
With laughter like sunshine, they flit and they soar,
In a world of their making, who could ask for more?

Cadence of the Conifers

A squirrel plays the violin, oh dear,
While wise old owls sip on root beer.
Nutty notes twist in the bright blue sky,
Dodging acorns as the breezes fly.

Branches sway and sway to the tune,
Rabbits hop along, dancing soon.
A chorus of frogs croaks out the bass,
Making merry in this leafy place.

Crunchy leaves join in on the fun,
As chipmunks race, saying, "Let's run!"
A cacophony of giggles spills,
In the green realm of the dancing hills.

Tune in, oh friends, to the woodland glee,
Where every creature sings carefree.
We'll swap our woes for a joyful cheer,
In the concert of conifers, come here!

Voices in the Twilight Grove

In twilight's glow, the frogs compose,
With the sneaky crickets stealing the shows.
A raccoon adds some flair of delight,
Wearing sunglasses, quite a sight!

The shadows dance as owls take flight,
Whispering secrets of the night.
But a clumsy hare trips over a stone,
Landing with grace, perfectly prone.

The fireflies flash, a light-hearted crew,
As chirpy conversations come into view.
And wise old trees chuckle loud,
At every bizarre bird in the crowd.

So raise a twig, let's toast in the gloam,
To the characters who brighten our home.
With laughter and song, come sing with me,
Under the lanterns of each leafy spree!

Songs of the Whispering Pines

Pines hum low in the afternoon sun,
As playful winds whirl, races begun.
A woodpecker drums, quite the maestro,
While a beaver takes notes, don't you know?

Caterpillars waltz on a soft, green leaf,
While ants hold a parade, above belief.
The chatter of birds' gossip fills the air,
As they twist and twirl without a care.

A squirrel in shades orders its meal,
"Make it acorn with a side of zeal!"
In this grove, nothing's ever mundane,
With every creature part of the refrain.

So listen closely, take a chance,
Join in the merriment, join the dance!
The songs of the pines, a whimsical sound,
In our secret world where joy's always found.

Rhapsody in the Thick of Trees

Beneath the boughs where the wild things sing,
A motley crew makes the forest swing.
A hedgehog in heels, a bear with a hat,
Their jam session is quite where it's at!

The tune bounces like a jumping flea,
As badgers sway like a bended knee.
A parade of critters joins in the fun,
With a twirling fox, oh what a run!

Branches shake with laughter and clapping,
A chorus of nature perfectly mapping.
Amidst the rhythm, they share a jest,
Under the canopy, feeling quite blessed.

So come one, come all, to the woodland show,
With shades drawn low and a gentle glow.
We'll rhapsodize 'neath our leafy retreat,
In this crazy symphony, can't be beat!

Nestled Notes in the Canopy

In the branches where they chatter,
A squirrel thinks it's a matter.
With acorns tossed and laughter shared,
While birds just sing, a little scared.

They hop and flap, a real charade,
Beneath the shade, their plans are laid.
One bird slips, causes such a fumble,
Then all explode in joyful tumble.

A gopher pops his head to see,
What's all this ruckus, wild and free?
With a wink, he tunes his ear,
And giggles softly, full of cheer.

They serenade the sleepy sun,
While ants march past, a busy run.
In the canopy, there's glee galore,
Each note a laugh, we couldn't ask for more!

Serenades of the Swaying Boughs

In the breeze, the branches sway,
Help me, help me, sing today!
A robin cracks a wonky joke,
While wrens around begin to poke.

With twirls and spins upon the wind,
Their harmony, a twisty trend.
A cat below looks up with glee,
"Those notes are simply crazy, me!"

The colors flash, the feathers whirl,
As every chirp makes nature twirl.
A dance of joy, in sync they sing,
Where laughter blooms, like bowing spring.

Then suddenly, a gusty air,
Leaves them bobbing without a care.
They laugh it off and take a bow,
At nature's fun, they're laughing now!

Chants of the Forest Flock

Underneath the leafy roof,
The birds all gather, seeking proof.
As one begins to gleefully shout,
The chorus joins, with more about.

A pecky tune bounces all around,
Echoed loudly from the ground.
Nearby rabbits stop to stare,
"Those sound like bubbles in the air!"

With flappy wings and tiny feet,
It's a laughter fest, a poppin' beat.
A finch in plaid dresses up with flair,
While all the others gasp and stare.

Their rhythmic chants raise up the sky,
Pigeons waddle in, "Oh my, oh my!"
Joined in fun, they roundly croon,
Making mischief, morning to noon!

Lullabies in Leafy Shadows

As twilight creeps and shadows grow,
A nightingale remembers so.
In whispers soft, he shares his song,
Of playful days when all feels wrong.

With every note, a giggle flows,
Through the dark, where humor glows.
A hedgehog joins with a little sigh,
"Keep it down! You're too spry!"

Owls chuckle, "What a silly show!
A midnight jam, let's steal the glow!"
With hoots and howls, they start to sway,
In leafy shadows, they dance and play.

As sleep descends and eyelids droop,
The forest sings, a merry troop.
Lullabies stitched with laughs so bright,
Through moonlit leaves, all feels just right!

Vibrations of the Verdant Veil

In a tree so tall, a bird starts to dance,
Wobbling its body, it gives folks a glance.
With a boisterous chirp, it flaps and it twirls,
And all of the squirrels just giggle and swirls.

Feathers in a frenzy, it starts to sing loud,
A tune so silly, it draws quite a crowd.
Bouncing on branches, it leaps here and there,
Why do birds try to dance in midair?

Worms start to wiggle, they're shaking with bliss,
They've never seen moves that could get them this is!
The sparrows start laughing; the jaybirds all jive,
In this leafy disco, all creatures arrive.

Oh the fun is contagious, the air is a buzz,
Every twig and twiglet's caught up in this fuzz.
With branches a-shaking, and laughter that swells,
The verdant veil echoes with humor so well.

Echoing Enchantment in Wooden Halls

In the wooden halls where shadows play,
A raven cracked jokes in its own funny way.
With a caw and a cackle, it made all heads turn,
As squirrels spilt acorns, they laughed and they learned.

A parrot sat nearby, with a real flair,
Every line it repeated elicited a stare.
"Who's the silliest bird? Bet you can't guess!"
They giggled and chirped, oh such a delight, no stress!

Pigeons piled high, they formed a tight crew,
Attempting to dance, but they wobbled on cue.
With every stumble, more laughter would rise,
As they flapped and tripped 'neath the verdant skies.

In wooden halls echoed a symphony bright,
Of jesters in feathers, a merry night flight.
As darkness enveloped, the giggles grew bold,
This banquet of laughs is a joy to behold.

Sonorous Shadows at Sunset

As the sun dipped low, the shadows grew long,
A quirky old owlet was singing a song.
With wise little hoots mixed with hiccups and squeaks,
He entertained all with his humorous peaks.

The robins joined in with a raucous refrain,
Their polished duet made the dusk feel like rain.
Each note a tickle, each sound a delight,
The woodland erupted in pure laughter's flight.

A frog leaped nearby, jumping high with a croak,
"Try to keep up!" he yelled in sheer joke.
But the more that they tried, the funnier it got,
As trees joined in laughter, how could they not?

With the moon casting shadows, the night was alive,
They danced to their music, how they would thrive!
In this sonorous twilight, no worries to fret,
When nature's a riot, you'll never forget.

The Language of Loyal Leaves

In the rustling leaves hides a cheeky crew,
Chirping and giggling as breezes blew through.
"Hey, look at that branch! I claim it as mine!"
Said a sprightly young finch, wearing leaves like a shrine.

With gossip and chatter, the petals do sway,
As branches crack jokes in a leafy ballet.
"Knock, knock!" said the pine; "Who's there?" cried the oak,
"Leaf who?" "Leaf me alone!" elicited a yoke.

The lilac and lily exchanged silly tales,
Of admirers who'd flutter but always would fail.
Every branch was a witness, their faces were bright,
As they giggled together with gleeful delight.

So next time you wander beneath the green dome,
Listen close to the laughter; you might find a home.
In the language of leaves, something funny exists,
A cacophony of chuckles that's hard to resist.

Soprano Shadows at Twilight

In twilight's glow, the voices rise,
Chirpy notes, a sweet surprise.
Feathers fluffed, they dance with glee,
Who knew that birds could sing off-key?

Each shadow flits with style and flair,
One even lands upon a hare.
While all around the critters stare,
Thinking, 'What's that tune to share?'

A cat nearby begins to prance,
But birds just laugh, they love to dance.
With acrobatics in the air,
The feathered troupe has naught a care!

As day gives way to evening's shroud,
They sound off, boisterous and loud.
Each note a tease, each chirp a jest,
At twilight's show, they are the best!

Vibrant Whistles of the Canopy

Up high where the air is bright and sweet,
A choir sings with wiggly feet.
They peek at squirrels, the cheeky crew,
Who marvel at melodies, oh so new!

With plucky beaks and a joyful cheer,
They serenade all who dare come near.
A raindrop falls, and oh what fun,
The birds just squeak, 'We'll never run!'

A tune for the skies, a laugh in the breeze,
The leafy giant sways with ease.
The critters bob in time to the song,
Under the canopy, where all belong!

Their vibrant whistles fill the air,
While nature giggles without a care.
As twilight whispers secrets low,
The birds just chuckle, 'Ready, set, go!'

Flight and Flourish in the Emerald

In emerald heights, with a joyful swoop,
Feathered friends form quite the troop.
They twirl and twist in the evening light,
Pretending they're stars taking flight!

Chasing shadows, what a sight to behold,
With plumes of colors, both bright and bold.
A misstep here, a hiccup there,
'Hey, catch me!' echoes in the air.

Each little chirp, a jolly tease,
To rustling leaves, an air-filled breeze.
With every flap, they spark delight,
A merry laughter takes to flight!

They play a game of hide and seek,
Though often caught, they just squeak,
'In emerald realms, we'll always play,
Come join our fun, won't you stay?'

Nature's Choir in the Twilight

As sun dips low, the choir sings,
Fluffy notes on caffeine wings.
A solo chirp, then all align,
'This is our time, it's birdie wine!'

Pecking about the boughs they share,
A stage of branches they will bare.
With each performance, giggles grow,
And all the critters clap, 'Bravo!'

Twilight's fun, their antics shine,
As crickets join, and frogs refine.
One bird tripped, in a twisty nest,
Said, 'Next act needs to cut the jest!'

In twilight's hush, their laughter spills,
Echoes of joy, and sweetened thrills.
With nature's choir, they take the prize,
Radiant smiles in night's disguise!

The Symphony of Solitary Flights

In the trees, the chatter flows,
With squawks and chirps like comedy shows.
Feathers fluff and tails all wag,
As they perform their mighty brag.

One takes off, a flapping mess,
While another lands in pure distress.
They strut and preen, with all their flair,
In their own world, without a care.

A worm is caught, the crowd goes wild,
They cheer and hoot like a beaming child.
Yet when they trip, oh what a sight,
The stage is set for pure delight.

In skies above, they flit and glide,
Mistakes abound, with laughter as their guide.
Oh, the choirs sing through branches tight,
Nature's humor, a true delight.

Crescendo of Celestial Creatures

Amidst the boughs, a starling slips,
Into a dance with wild arm flips.
The beat is set, a flurry of fun,
When beaks collide under the sun.

The finch tries to lead, but oh, what grace!
Trips on a twig, but keeps up the pace.
They giggle and chirp in jovial glee,
Each blunder a mark of comedy.

Twists and turns in flighty display,
Feathers ruffled, but they don't sway.
Dodging each other like ducks in a line,
Squeaks, squawks, and beeps—all intertwined.

As daylight dims, the giggles won't cease,
A cacophony of laughter increases.
In the dusky hue, mischief will reign,
Their playful antics, never in vain.

Songs of Freedom upon the Foliage

A little fellow with a big ol' voice,
Sings of crickets, claiming it's his choice.
He whistles tunes that wiggle and warp,
As trees chuckle softly, all seem to snort.

The chattering chorus, a warbling spree,
Songs of all flavors, quite the jamboree.
Each note a giggle, each chord a smile,
They celebrate freedom in their own style.

An owl hoots loud, "That's not how it goes!"
The finchers reply, striking silly poses.
"Just try to follow, you wise old bird!"
But his laughter joins, so none are deterred.

Leaves sway with rhythm, a leafy dance cue,
As mischief and melody drift on the dew.
Nature's stage covered in laughter so sweet,
The songs of the brave, brighten their beat.

Echoes from the Cedar Sanctuary

In the shelter of trees, a ruckus starts,
A cacophony of trills fills the hearts.
One haughty crow, soaring high,
Tells the tale of a clumsy fly.

Pecking and prancing, what a grand jest,
The sparrows zoom by, putting it to test.
A clattering chorus, full of delight,
Echoes of humor in morning light.

A jay lands awkward, a sight to behold,
His pride deflated, he's no longer bold.
The company erupts into roars of cheer,
For laughter amongst them is always near.

As dusk settles in and shadows grow long,
They sing of the day—a whimsical song.
Though feathers may ruffle and egos might trip,
The sanctuary thrives on their playful quip.

Nature's Untold Harmonies

In the trees, a chatter flows,
A squirrel dances, and everyone knows.
The robins giggle, the jays squawk loud,
As the shy old owl grins, feeling very proud.

A woodpecker taps, a beat so fine,
While raccoons plot to steal your lunch divine.
The fluttering wings, a sight to behold,
Nature's band plays, with antics bold.

Chirps and trills paint the air,
With every note, a feathered flare.
Funny sounds make the branches sway,
As the leaves join in on this playful ballet.

Caterpillars twist, creating a scene,
While ladybugs waltz, looking pristine.
In this wooded stage, all take part,
With laughter echoing, nature's art.

Lull in the Leafy Canopy

Beneath the canopy, a cozy nook,
A frog croaks loudly, writing a book.
The brook giggles, splashing bright,
While ants march on, in their tiny flight.

Ladybugs play tag on the bark,
While chipmunks juggle nuts in the dark.
The breeze whispers secrets to the vine,
As turtles huddle, enjoying sunshine.

Grasshoppers leap, showing off their skills,
While hedgehogs chuckle, sharing their thrills.
The chorus of whimsy, in the trees,
Makes even the hardest critics feel pleased.

A lullaby echoes in leaves so green,
Nature's performance, like none we've seen.
With giggles and chirps, the world spins slow,
Creating a calm of delightful flow.

Ballads of the Beneath

Down in the soil, where secrets lie,
Worms compose tunes as they gently sigh.
The beetles march, with rhythm so grand,
While moles tell tales of the underground band.

Rooted deep, the trees tap along,
To the chirpy tweets of creatures strong.
As ants hold meetings, plotting their dance,
In this underground world, they take a chance.

A critter parade, everything's neat,
With earth's own beats, they stomp their feet.
The laughter of toads adds to the cheer,
While all join in, no room for fear.

With every wiggle, the ground resonates,
Nature's odd ballads, oh how it vibrates!
From underground layers, fun melodies rise,
In the heart of the earth, joy never dies.

The Glistening Aria

Amidst the branches, a shimmer bursts,
With insects humming, and frogs' funny bursts.
The sun shines down, casting playful rays,
While the leaves twirl, in whimsical ways.

A dance of colors, nature's attire,
As bees sway gently, like a live choir.
The flowers giggle, all in bloom,
Spreading laughter, dispelling the gloom.

Hummingbirds zip, with precision and flair,
Making mischief, as if they don't care.
Mice start a conga, right on the ground,
In this joyful chaos, laughter abounds.

With every flutter, notes fill the sky,
Creating an aria, as time passes by.
Nature's concert, filled with delight,
Bringing smiles, from morning to night.

Seraphim of the Shade

In the branches, chatter flies,
Feathers ruffle, oh what a surprise!
One thinks it's Shakespeare's chat,
While another's stuck in a silly hat.

A squirrel joins in, nuts in tow,
Claims he's a star in their show.
While the sun peeks through the green,
A peanut dance starts, it's quite the scene!

With wormy jokes that twist and twirl,
They laugh and twist, oh what a whirl!
Nature's stage is quite absurd,
Who knew that trees could host a bird?

So join the fun in the leafy nook,
Be part of this rustic, raucous book.
With caws and calls, we sing all day,
In this shady circus, come out and play!

Voices that Paint the Sky

A chorus of squeaks and silly tweets,
We gather for our morning retreats.
Miss Finch brings pastries, oh what delight,
But Mr. Grackle steals one, what a sight!

"Hey! That's my muffin!" the finch does squawk,
As the news spreads like a rumor on rock.
The warbler sings of sweet revenge,
While the woodpecker drums on an old stone bench.

Among the branches, tunes arise,
Every chirp is a sweet surprise.
They harmonize with plucky flair,
Dancing under the sun's golden glare.

With luck, we'll find the best of fun,
As the day wraps up and we are done.
So raise your beaks and join in the sky,
Where laughter reigns and dreams fly high!

Rhythms of the Rustic Boughs

In the glen where shadows sway,
Birds break into a zany ballet.
Ducks quack a beat, and frogs start to croak,
While the drumming of woodpeckers makes me choke!

The freedom of song beneath the boughs,
Is filled with pranks and giggles—oh wow!
A jay just tripped and fell off a perch,
Now he's planning a "birdie" research!

Feathers fly as they take wing,
Jokes flit around like a song on a string.
"Why did the chicken cross?" they tease,
"To show the platypus it was at ease!"

From dawn to dusk, they strut and play,
Creating joy in every way.
So join the ruckus, let laughter flow,
In the leafy equipped orchestra's show!

Celestial Chorus of the Glades

In a glade where echoes twirl,
Feathered friends make oddity whirl.
One sings opera while the other snores,
Creating laughter that soars and soars!

The rabbit hops to the tune's sweet twist,
While the owl's head turns with a fussy list.
"Whooo needs pizzazz?" he hoots in the shade,
"This melody is free and homemade!"

With a croaky croon, the frog steals the show,
"Ribbit! Ribbit! I too can blow!"
As a breeze tickles notes that prance in air,
The insects buzz—what a wild affair!

Under star-studded skies, they keep it bright,
Creating a symphony throughout the night.
So join this raucous, starry discourse,
In the glades where our laughter's a force!

Echoing Hearts in the Verdant

In the treetops, a chirp and a cheer,
Feathers ruffle, the jokes disappear.
A robin slips on dew, oh what a sight,
Dancing on branches, a feathery flight.

The owl turns its head, what was that sound?
A squirrel in stilettos, so proud, so profound.
With acorns as maracas, it shakes with glee,
A party of critters, come join, set us free!

A chorus of giggles, the trees start to sway,
A blue jay in shades, he's here for the play.
With a wink and a squawk, he leads the parade,
As worms in the grass shake off their charade.

The sun dips low, painting laughter in light,
With jokes on the breezes, what a delight!
Echoes of joy swirl through leaves green and bright,
Nature's own cackle, taking off in flight.

Harmony in Hushed Nooks

In the shade of the willows, a chat takes a turn,
With whispering breezes that make the leaves churn.
A finch tells a tale, all twisted and funny,
While her friends roll their eyes, as bright as the sunny.

A chattering squirrel, with nuts stashed in bags,
Tries to start a band with a crow and her rags.
The harmonies clash, oh what a racket,
As frogs join the choir with a big croaking racket!

The chipmunks are laughing, they can't keep it straight,
A woodpecker's rhythm is never first-rate.
Yet each little critter has a tune to reveal,
In corners of quiet where laughter can heal.

With nooks full of giggles, the harmony swells,
The rustling leaves hum like their own jolly bells.
Nestled in laughter, the world feels just right,
Underneath starry skies that twinkle by night.

Ballads of the Forest Floor

Down on the forest floor, a concert unfolds,
With beetles in tuxedos and tales to be told.
A caterpillar croons while he shimmies along,
Each note a slippery rhyme in this woodland song.

The toad joins in, with a bass so profound,
Croaking beneath trees where the laughter abounds.
The mushrooms are grooving, all painted and bold,
As grasshoppers breakdance, their moves uncontrolled!

The snails in the back attempt the moonwalk,
While fireflies flash signals that say, "Let's rock!"
With glittery slippers and glimmering shells,
The night whispers secrets; it's magic that dwells.

Outrageous and merry, they sing through the night,
With each little giggle, the shadows take flight.
Their ballads of joy spread like ripples in air,
On the forest floor, they dance without care.

Symphony of the Woodland Path

On a woodland path, where the sunlight plays,
A rabbit's off-key in a mash-up of rays.
With a hop and a skip, he finds his own groove,
Making music with twigs, he's got something to prove.

A deer prances by, with her friends in tow,
They twirl to the tune of a soft, soothing flow.
While turtles in slippers rock steady in place,
A band of the oddest; they win in this race!

A fox shoots on by, with a sly little glance,
Joining in laughter as they all make a dance.
With each little stumble, they chuckle and grin,
In the symphony made from the joy deep within.

As shadows stretch long, the sun starts to fade,
This woodland orchestra is nature's own parade.
Together they harmonize, so merry and bright,
A symphony ensues as they fade into night.

Songs of Solace in the Thicket

In the thicket where the critters play,
A squirrel sings about his nut buffet.
The fox joins with a slightly off-beat,
While the owl hoots, trying to keep discreet.

The rabbit hops with a little jig,
Hiding from the cat, not quite so big.
They laugh and cheer, under branches thick,
In this leafy world, their tunes are quick.

A hawk overhead, a judge of sound,
Mocks the music, while whirling 'round.
But down below, the earthworms groove,
To the rhythm of roots, they happily move.

So raise your voice, sing out your cheer,
In the thicket with friends, there's nothing to fear.
As melodies mingle, both strange and sweet,
Nature's shoulders sway to the offbeat treat.

Melodies from the Mystic Wood

In the mystic wood where shadows dance,
The woodpecker's tapping starts the prance.
A deer takes a bow, showing off her grace,
While the raccoon giggles, keeping pace.

The mushrooms hum with a squishy song,
Chanting tales of right and wrong.
A porcupine joins, with quills held high,
As a lizard croons a trying lullaby.

Through branches we swing, on vines we zoom,
Unbothered by worries that often loom.
The bullfrogs croak in a comedic tune,
Turning twilight into a lively afternoon.

So let's gather round, with laughter to spare,
In this wood of wonders, let's dance without care.
For each hearty laugh, every glitch in the beat,
Makes our escapades taste a little more sweet.

Harmonious Wanderings through Nature's Realm

Through nature's realm, we roam and sway,
With melodies swirling, brightening the gray.
A beaver hums as he shapes his dam,
While a lark shouts, 'Hey, look at me, fam!'

The dragonflies dart with a zippy refrain,
Wheeling as if they're quite insane.
A grumpy old badger grumbles a beat,
While the butterflies twirl, looking ten times sweet.

The brook babbles on with an eager flair,
While the sunbeams twinkle, catching every glare.
Each ripple and rustle adds to the fun,
As critters pile on, one by one.

So come join the song, in this vibrant space,
Laughing and hopping with joy in our face.
With each little note and each hop and swirl,
We make nature a stage, come dance, give it a whirl!

Sibilant Sounds in the Shade

In the shade where the whispers play,
Chirpy chatter fills the day.
The lizard, lounging, tells a tall tale,
While a snail hums sweetly, slow and frail.

A bee buzzes with a comical drone,
As the dragonflies wink from their cactus throne.
A chattering magpie steals the spotlight,
While the leaves rustle, fueling the delight.

Echoes of fun in the leafy choir,
With frisky squirrels sparking the fire.
They laugh at the cat, who plots and schemes,
While dreaming a snooze in dappled beams.

So join in the fun, let your laughter soar,
In the shade we find joy, forevermore.
With each silly chirp and each whimsical call,
Nature reminds us, we're all one and all.

Twilight Flights and Trilling Hearts

In twilight's soft and hazy glow,
The feathered jesters dip and flow.
With silly hops and cheeky peeps,
They dance and tease while daylight sleeps.

A chirp, a tweet, a squawking tune,
They gather 'round like leaves in June.
With flapping wings and ruffled chests,
They claim the skies, the feathery jest.

Oh, watch them dive, they flap, they swirl,
A show-off here, a twirler there.
They wink and nod, such funny sights,
Creating laughter through the nights.

As stars peek out and giggles blend,
In playful serenades, they send.
With every trill, a tale unfolds,
Of feathered dreams that dare be bold.

Lullabies of the Evergreen Grove

In the woods where pine trees sway,
A chorus hums at the end of day.
With plucky notes and silly grins,
They croon to bugs and tiny kin.

Underneath the branches wide,
They gather close and sing with pride.
A warble here, a snicker there,
In this grove, naught but good cheer.

They chat of worms and twinkling flies,
With tales that make the saplings cry.
A giggle fits, they can't hold still,
Creating tunes as sweet as thrill.

So close your eyes, feel the delight,
As laughter rings through the soft night.
In harmony, they paint the dark,
With lullabies that leave a mark.

Wings that Write the Wind

With wings that flap like comical pens,
They scribble stories where laughter begins.
With loops and dives, they twist and twirl,
Creating chaos in the swirling whirl.

A cotton cloud, a plushy seat,
Where chortles echo and heartbeats greet.
With every glide, a giggle flies,
In the air, their mischief lies.

Oh, the tales of tangled nests,
Of mixed-up eggs and feathery quests.
From treetop leaps to dance-filled springs,
They sketch the wind with joyful wings.

Their stories carried on sweet night air,
Of pranks and stunts and bold affairs.
For every flap, a clownish cheer,
In laughter's wind, they disappear.

Notes from a Hidden Glade

In hidden glades where soft winds flow,
The merry chirpers steal the show.
With quick little hops and pecks so slight,
They prank the shadows in the fading light.

With notes that jiggle and wiggle too,
They charm the flowers, the bees, and you!
A flutter here, a hop and spin,
In every tune, you can hear their grin.

Oh, watch them share their secret scheme,
As daisies nod and crickets beam.
Each note a silly joke or prank,
As smiles grow large and spirits tank.

With whispers sweet as cookies baked,
Their music dances, laughter faked.
So join the fun as night takes hold,
In hidden glades where joy is bold.

Soft Strains from the Thicket

In the thicket, chirps abound,
A feathered clown on a merry round.
He flaps his wings, quite out of tune,
Dancing around like a silly cartoon.

With a wink and a nod, he starts to prance,
In a twirl and a whirl, he leads the dance.
A chorus of giggles from branches so high,
While leaves shake their heads, oh my, oh my!

Music Unfurling in the Breezes

Through the branches, laughter flies,
With each note, the old trunk sighs.
A raspy tune, quite off the mark,
Yet every tree joins in with a spark.

The sky chuckles, the clouds draw near,
Putting on a show for the unsuspecting deer.
A symphony of chaos, sweet and absurd,
As nature gathers for this silly word.

Chorus of the Green-Cloaked

In cloaks of green, they gather near,
Chirping jokes that only they'll hear.
One mimics a cat, the other a frog,
Their concert starts at the hour of the fog.

With beaks wide open, they crack some jokes,
The laughter spreads among old oaks.
Each zany note a feathered jest,
A greenside giggle, truly the best!

Trills on the Wind-Swept Bough

On swaying boughs, the jesters vie,
In a tangle of trills and a twist of sighs.
Each note a poke, a playful tease,
As they flap about in the gentle breeze.

The winds carry tales of their grand display,
With giggles that echo throughout the day.
Oh, to be a bird, with such crazy flair,
Dancing on branches without a care!

Crescendo of the Canopies

Up in the trees, a ruckus blares,
Chirps and flaps, a chorus of dares.
Feathers aflutter, in comical spins,
A dance-off begins, who loses? Who wins?

Squirrels peek in, with popcorn in tow,
They laugh at the sight of a feathered show.
A warbler's on stage, doing the twist,
The crowd goes wild, who could resist?

A jay cracks jokes, wearing a crown,
With a raucous caw, he steals the crown.
The audience roars, it's party galore,
Can birds hold their drinks? We're eager for more!

As sunset paints gold on each feathered face,
The fun doesn't stop; it's an endless chase.
With a final bow, they settle the score,
Tomorrow's another—what's in store once more?

A Symphony of Fluttering Fables

In a bush, a robin tells tales so sly,
About a badger who thought he could fly.
With a flap and a flap, oh, how he did try,
But he bumped his head, oh me, oh my!

A finch in the back starts snickering loud,
'You should've seen it, he flopped like a cloud!'
The laughter erupts, and the tales grow tall,
About the time a fox tripped over a ball.

Then comes a wren, with a shy little grin,
'Remember that owl? He danced in a spin!'
The crowd falls silent, in fits of delight,
Imagining owls in neon at night.

As twilight descends, and the fables take flight,
They bid each other goodnight with pure light.
In the symphony's grace, the giggles will stay,
For tomorrow they'll return, in a feathered ballet.

Whispers of the Whispering Willows

In the willows, whispers flutter and tease,
A parrot complains, 'I'm just sick of the bees!'
They buzz in my ears, I'm ready to flee,
If they touch my wings, they'll end up with me!

Chickadees giggle, 'You should wear some shades,
Dazzle them with colors, it'll drive them in spades!'
The parrot nods slow, in a comical plight,
'Next time I'll bring sequins, we'll do it just right!'

A sparrow flies in, with a witty remark,
'You should just tell them, "Buzz off!" in the park!'
Laughter erupts, it's a hilarious jest,
As the willows shake off their leafy behest.

The whispers continue, like breezes so fleet,
While the birds celebrate with a snack and a beat.
In the heart of the woods, where the giggles unwind,
A concert of chuckles is tailored to mind.

Rhapsody of the Resilient Pines

In a grove of pines, a chatterhouse brews,
Where puns flow and laughter is always the news.
A pinecone's the judge of a roguish debate,
Who's the best singer? Let's hurry, don't wait!

A thrush cracks a joke about seeds and their fate,
While a tall, solemn owl joins in, looking great.
With wisdom and wit, he gives quite a fright,
'You're all out of tune, but I find it quite right!'

The woodpecker rat-a-tats to keep the beat,
While young saplings sway to the rhythm and heat.
Who knew that the pines would host such a show?
The laughter cascades like a bright, feathered bow.

As night settles softly, with stars peering down,
They applaud each other, each feathered clown.
Tomorrow we'll gather, under branches so fine,
In a rhapsody's spirit, let's toast with some wine!

Melodies in the Mist

In the trees, the chirps collide,
Squirrels dance with fluffy pride,
A jay squawks, a mocking jest,
Every note, a feathered quest.

Dew drops sparkle, tunes ensue,
Worms below are singing too,
A thrush trips on a fallen twig,
Then laughs at his own silly gig.

The Crows compete, a raucous show,
While woodpeckers play tic-tac-toe,
With hoots and tweets, the breezes shift,
Nature's stage, a lively gift.

As the sun peeks through the fog,
A chorus rises, sheer dialogue,
With a wink and a twist, they sing,
In this giddy woodland fling.

Echoes of Forest Harmonies

A robin lost its little tune,
As it tried a jig beneath the moon,
The owls chuckle, soft and low,
While crickets keep the tempo slow.

Old trees sway with laughter bright,
As branches dance in sheer delight,
A lark does flips, a sight to see,
While ants tap feet, oh so free!

The badger plucks a ballad's note,
Chasing fireflies, up they float,
With every sound, the woods awake,
Who knew that rhymes could make you quake?

Through the laughter, echoes weave,
An audience of leaves believe,
With every chirp, the tales unfold,
In this mischief, joy is bold.

Feathered Serenades at Dawn

At dawn the feathery fools arrive,
Pigeons prance, they jive and dive,
A parrot shows his funny face,
As squirrels storm the coffee space.

A warbler drops his morning bread,
With every crumb, the gossip spread,
With cackles, caws, and silly squawks,
While rabbits join in earnest talks.

A finch in stripes, all bright and spry,
Composes tunes that float the sky,
With rhymes of grass and silly blunders,
The world awakens to their wonders.

A chorus builds, a comic cast,
As morning brings a joyful blast,
In the skies, a raucous band,
Where laughter echoes across the land.

Voices of the Woodland Choir

A choir formed of beak and wing,
With every chirp, the forest sings,
The jests they make, like whispers spry,
As branches wave and spirits fly.

A fox curls up, his ears a perk,
Debating whether to join their quirk,
The woodpecker dons a hat so grand,
In this silly show, all humor planned.

With each note, the world grows bright,
As creatures gather, pure delight,
With giggles echoing through the pines,
The woodland choir makes funny lines.

So gather 'round, hear every jest,
Nature's laughter is truly the best,
From limbs and leaves, their joy can't tire,
In this sweet woodland, laughter—our choir.

Soaring Stanzas Under the Stars

In the treetops, a ruckus abound,
Feathered pals chatter, making silly sounds.
One thinks he's a star, the others don't care,
They all start to dance, with moves quite rare.

Wings flapping wildly, they giggle and glide,
A chorus of chuckles from every side.
One attempts a flip, but oh, what a mess,
Tangled up branches, in feathered distress!

A squirrel joins in, with acrobat flair,
Balance is key, but the clouds give a scare.
They laugh as they tumble, no care for the fall,
Under the moonlight, they frolic, enthralled.

So the night carries on, with each joyful screech,
A reminder that fun is the best kind of speech.
In the treetops, the jests never end,
With each hoot and caw, they uplift and mend.

Harmonies from the Hollowed Bark

Nestled in shadows, where mischief's afoot,
A rascally gang in a tree trunk so cute.
They peek out and giggle, pulling great pranks,
With acorns for bombs, they fill up the ranks.

One sly little fellow, with feathers all bright,
Tries to sing scales, but he's off in mid-flight.
His pals start a chorus, a cacophony loud,
As they cheer on their friend, proudly feeling so proud.

The bark starts to wobble, as laughter takes hold,
A bumblebee joins, turning brave and bold.
"Buzzing is better than flapping," he sings,
And everyone giggles at all of their flings.

From hollowed-out trees, their melodies rise,
A humor-filled symphony under the skies.
In this jolly circus of cheer and delight,
The harmony shines through the dark of the night.

Gentle Voices of the Green Canopy

A chorus of chirrups in soft leafy beds,
Where laughter erupts from their pint-sized heads.
Up high on the branches, they plot and they scheme,
With wild, goofy antics that feel like a dream.

"Look at me!" yells one, "I'm a hawk, bold and grand!"
But instead slips and falls, landing right on the sand.
His friends burst in laughter, with feathers askew,
"Next time just stick to your chirping, it's true!"

A wise old owl, perched way out of sight,
Chuckles to himself at this pitiful plight.
"I may be the sage, and they may be absurd,
But life without joy is just simply unheard!"

So under the canopy, where mischief takes flight,
The giggles and giggles dance stars into night.
In the boughs, they unite, making memories wide,
Their gentle communication, in nature, in stride.

The Enchanted Anthem

From dawn until dusk, they serenade trees,
With whimsical tunes carried on the breeze.
One dreams of a world where they're opera kings,
But often erupts into silly little flings.

The tallest of them, with a shiny green hat,
Sways and spins wildly, saying, "Look at that!"
He loses his balance, then lands with a thud,
While others just cackle, rolling soft in the mud.

With echoes of laughter, they tumble about,
A merry band of rascals, their joy leaves no doubt.
The leaves gently rustle, joining in on their cheer,
Each chorus of lightness is music to hear.

And as dusk approaches with stars in the sky,
These merry little minstrels continue to fly.
With antics and melodies forever enshrined,
Their enchanted anthem brings laughter to mind.

Meadow's Melodic Reverie

In glades where giggles flutter wide,
A chorus of chirps, oh how they glide,
With silly hops and a wobbly dance,
They tease the breeze with a merry prance.

Their beaks hold jokes and funny tunes,
Like feathered fools beneath the moons,
One trips on a twig, with a flapping shout,
And all the others can't help but pout.

Laughter echoes from leafy glen,
While one bird stumbles, then starts again,
Chasing shadows with flapping zest,
In this vibrant fable, they're simply the best!

As sunlight dapples the emerald floor,
The playful team just wants to soar,
They giggle at clouds, sway with the breeze,
In this merry meadow, they aim to please.

A Cadence of Feathered Dreams

High up in branches, a ruckus breaks,
A plucky duo plans for some pranks,
With a little hop and a cheeky wink,
They plot their moves by the river's brink.

One's a joker with a knack for surprise,
While the other fluffs up in disguise,
They squawk and flap, oh what a scene,
As they argue over whose turn to preen.

With feathers bobbing, they dance a jig,
Each feathery twist a wild little gig,
And while they laugh, a nearby dog,
Barks in rhythm, joining the fog.

Under the sky, their antics thrive,
With every chirp, the world feels alive,
In a flutter of joy, they find their bliss,
For who would trade such a feathery kiss?

Fluttering Revelations from the Trees

Among the branches, a ruckus is heard,
As one little chirp attempts to be heard,
He shares his thoughts on the meaning of flights,
While others debate his wild bird sights.

With flapping wings and curious beaks,
They jest and giggle, the humor peaks,
A lecture on worms gets hilariously wrong,
As one bird forgets the words to their song.

Round and round in their feathery hall,
They flutter and tumble, they can't feel small,
A joke about cats sends them in tears,
In this tree of laughter, they chase all fears.

So join the revels where fun takes flight,
With feathers aflutter, all day and night,
In a dance of delight and a cheerful refrain,
These trees are the stage for their joyous campaign.

Trills Among the Twisted Branches

A merry band flits amid the leaves,
Making music that teasingly weaves,
With twists and turns, they flaunt their flair,
Creating rhythms that dance in the air.

One tries to sing, but hits all the wrong notes,
While others burst into laughter, afloat like boats,
With silly trills and a comical squawk,
They strut their antics right past the flock.

In the sun-dappled shade, they wiggle their toes,
Chasing each other, like children they pose,
A flurry of feathers, a wild parade,
Through the twisted branches, their jokes cascade.

So let the trees echo with cackles and glee,
For in their silly world, life's as bright as can be,
They'll trill and they'll chirp, share a laugh or two,
Amongst the green chaos, there's joy to pursue.

www.ingramcontent.com/pod-product-compliance
Lightning Source LLC
Chambersburg PA
CBHW071836160426
43209CB00003B/323